Top 13 Secrets To Success in Life & Business

Steve Jobs

The Power Of Think Different

EF_EntrepreneurshipFacts.com

Warning-Disclaimer!

The purpose of this book is to educate and entertain. The author or publisher does not guarantee that anyone following the techniques, suggestions, tips, ideas, or strategies will become successful. The author and publisher shall have neither liability or responsibility to anyone with respect to any loss or damage caused or alleged to be caused, directly or indirectly by the information contained in this book.

All information contained within this book has been researched from reputable sources. If any information is found to be false, please contact the publisher, who will be happy to make corrtivections for future editions.

Follow EntrepreneurshipFacts on social media to stay updated with our free book promotions and increase your knowledge about business and successful people on a daily basis:

Instagram   Facebook   Twitter

Also check out our website for the latest facts and articles about business and entrepreneurship:

www.EntrepreneurshipFacts.com

Table of Contents

Introduction 6

Lesson #1 - Here's to the crazy ones. 9

Lesson #2 - Good artists copy, great artists steal. 20

Lesson #3 - I don't have any skeletons in my closet that can't be allowed out. 26

Lesson #4 - Do you want to come with me and change the world? 31

Lesson #5 - Just figure out what's next. 36

Lesson #6 - Just explore things. 42

Lesson #7 - Getting fired from Apple was the best thing that could have ever happened to me. 49

Lesson #8 - What separates successful entrepreneurs from the non-successful ones is pure perseverance. 53

Lesson #9 - Innovation distinguishes between a leader and a follower 59

Lesson #10 - You can't just ask customers what they want and then try to give that to them. 65

Lesson #11 - Being the richest man in the cemetery doesn't matter to me. 70

Lesson #12 - If today were the last day of my life, would I want to do what I am about to do today?'
.... 77

Lesson #13 - You can't connect the dots looking forward; you can only connect them looking backward.. 86

Conclusion 86

Introduction

As a true innovator, Steve Jobs made a huge impact and undoubtedly altered the way we view the world. From how we talk to each other and think about business, to the way we approach every facet of our daily life, the shift in our society is undeniable. As an inventive and innovative business genius, he was also committed to creating a positive impact, influencing the lives of others for the better. His success as Apple's co-founder and CEO, along with his role at Pixar will forever leave an impression in the minds of so many. Passing away at only 56, he left an impressive net worth of over $10 billion. It leaves us asking about the unknown...if he were still around today, what would he be accomplishing? What projects would he be working on? What kind of innovative and insightful feedback would he offer some of the issues we face in today's society?

From Ford's knack for efficiency to Edison's innovative mind or Disney's creative genius, Jobs undoubtedly falls among the ranks as some of the most innovative and extraordinary people in America's history. However, Jobs no doubt had negative aspects of his character as well. Those who know him would remember his demanding, sometimes aggressive approach. Regardless, what he will be remembered for in our society today is the way he aptly used his creativity and vision to forever transform the state of business and the use of technology in our daily lives.

As one of America's most well known people, Jobs

will remain in the record as someone who undoubtedly transformed how society would live in the future. Others would say he is a creative genius; regardless, Jobs had an undeniable aptitude for capturing the attention of his peers with his charm and a fervent passion for what he believed. Unsurprisingly, many of his words continue to be used, his distinct phrases remaining as renowned as the tangible products he created.

Throughout this book, we'll delve into the greater significance of these words. By analyzing the meaning of each phrase, we'll learn about a true story of Jobs, living his words and applying them to his daily life and the way he approached each business situation. We'll gain a greater understanding of who Steve Jobs was by looking into the things he said, the movements he instigated and the work he spurred on through his inspiring legacy.

Quote # 1

"Here's to the crazy ones — the misfits, the rebels, the troublemakers, the round pegs in the square holes. The ones who see things differently — they're not fond of rules. You can quote them, disagree with them, glorify or vilify them, but the only thing you can't do is ignore them because they change things. They push the human race forward, and while some may see them as the crazy ones, we see genius, because the ones who are crazy enough to think that they can change the world, are the ones who do."

Quote Context:

This quote is from the 1997 Apple Advertising Campaign "Think different." The campaign earned an Emmy for best commercial in 1998.

Get to know Jobs:

Jobs' approach, ideals and thirst for asking "why" made him a true innovator of his time. Considering both the era he lived in, and the culture that surrounded him, his drive to ask questions and challenge the status quo was simply remarkable.

Jobs was born in the mid 1950s, in San Francisco. His mother, a young, recently graduated woman was startled to find out she was pregnant. Feeling she had no choice but to give him up for adoption, she wanted to ensure he went to a good home. Upon finding an upper class, educated Catholic family, she chose this home for him, but was dismayed when this arrangement fell through, as they preferred a girl. Consequently, Paul and Clara Jobs agreed to adopt him. Upon finding out that the couple adopting her newborn were not college educated, she recanted and decided not to sign the adoption papers. Going as far as to head to the courts, after Paul and Clara committed to giving Steve a college education, she reluctantly agreed.

Jobs grew up in a healthy and loving home. Going as far to describe his biological parents as a "sperm and egg bank," he made no qualms about describing who he really believed his parents to be. Jobs got a new sister in 1957 when his parents made the choice to adopt a girl, Patricia. Jobs' father had a love for everything mechanical, and the two spend hours working on projects together, with Paul passing on whatever mechanical knowledge he could to his son. Jobs was in awe of his father's ability to fix anything, and build the most complicated of items with ease, and over the years developed his own strong love of electronics.

Although Jobs undoubtedly enjoyed the time spent with his father, working on a multitude of projects at home, he didn't fit in within the traditional setting of his school. Jobs' inquisitive nature, tendency to question everything, and out-of-the-box approach left teachers struggling to control him. At home, Jobs didn't receive the punishment that may have been levied by a more traditional parent. In his childhood, Jobs' father had been subject to abuse, and consequently avoided disciplining his son. Feeling unequipped to handle his suspensions, his father cast blame upon the school, claiming that they were unable to properly stimulate his clever and gifted son.

Jobs was relatively athletic, competing on the swim team, but predominantly avoided the world of team sports. One thing that did capture his attention was a club at his school called the Hewlett-Packard Explorer Club. Jobs listened in rapture to the engineers demonstrating both their products, and their deep expertise about the technology they were sharing. At the young age of twelve, he saw his first computer, and in the time that followed, he quickly grew a strong and unshakable love of the computer world.

Jobs' interest in computers continued to grow throughout his high school years. Located in the small center of Cupertino, he developed a number of friendships with classmates who shared his interests and passions. Jobs' girlfriend at the time, Chrisann Brennan, was artistically gifted and consequently had different interests. One of his friends, Steve Wozniak, was an engineering student. Although he was a few years older than Jobs, Wozniak, unlike Brennan, was someone with whom Jobs could discuss his passion for technology. Steve Jobs' girlfriend at the time, Chrisann Brennan, was artistically gifted, so

Wozniak, although a few years older than Jobs, was someone with which Jobs could discuss his passion for technology.

Even at this age, Jobs had remarkable initiative. During the completion of a school project with the Hewlett Packard Club, Jobs came across a situation where he didn't have the parts he wanted. Rather than find an alternative solution, Jobs connected with the owner of the plant, William Hewlett, and requested the appropriate parts. Not only did Hewlett provide the parts, but was so blown away by Jobs' initiative and drive that he presented him with the opportunity to come to Hewlett Packard plant for an internship the following summer.

After Jobs graduated from the Homestead High School in his modest hometown, he registered at Reed College in Portland, Oregon. While attending college was his biological mother's primary hope for him, Jobs continued to struggle in a traditional setting and dropped out halfway through the year. Although not officially enrolled, he continued to stay connected within the college, albeit with a non-traditional approach. Jobs took in a number of classes--from English courses exploring the works of Shakespeare or creatively-focused workshops like calligraphy, he also experimented with a number of drugs and continued to date his high-school girlfriend, Brennan.

Jobs went on to begin work at Atari in 1973, but it was short-lived. Quitting his job, he traveled to India with his friend Daniel Kottke. Planning to explore the world of Zen Buddhism, they expected the trip to be one of enlightenment and spiritual growth. While Jobs had previously delved into the world of Kainchi ashram with Neem Baba, Baba had sadly passed away the previous fall.

Determined to continue along this path, Jobs headed to Haidakhan Babaji ashram, where he'd spend two years. At the end of his impactful trip, Jobs returned to California with a shaved head and wearing traditional Indian clothing for months after his return.

Lesson from Steve Jobs:

The quote above indicates exactly what Jobs cared about, and what he made a priority in his life. It also provides insight into how he reflected on himself and his own aptitudes and talents. Through these words, Jobs saw himself as an outsider to the general populous. He was someone who would continuously challenge the status quo. He had an insatiable drive to both push others to question the way they thought, and to spur them on to do better. Woven throughout Jobs' story, there is a continuous and undeniable theme of not just tolerating this "different" way of looking at life, but learning to appreciate it. Throughout the years, Jobs seemed adamant in his quest for perfection, having a strong and growing frustration for individuals who he thought of as inferior, or who were unable to achieve the same standard. For those who strive to understand Jobs at a deeper level, they are often acutely aware of two personality traits that appear to run counter to each other. Jobs seemed to fly in the face of tradition and reject the rules, yet would pursue the elusive 'perfection' with a fervor one would expect from a much more conservative personality. However, this intriguing mix seemed to only increase the draw to understand him and delve deeper into what made him tick.

Jobs' "think different" approach presents itself again and again throughout his lifetime. In understanding him, it's essential to understand the depth of his personality traits. While he undoubtedly held creative and innovative thought in high esteem, he ironically would get frustrated and agitated by those whose values or thoughts didn't align.

Jobs had a deep appreciation of anything different, against the grain, or innovative. These deeply held values meant that taking calculated risks and continuously pushing the limits wasn't just tolerated, but things he strove for. Within his field, where innovation was expected, Jobs' style was a perfect fit. He held the strong belief that employees should continuously push the limits, refuse to conform to traditional expectations, and dare to challenge anyone. His grandiose visions and fervent passion for the next challenge led him to build a network of people who could buy-in to his vision or maybe had their own unconventional approach. With Jobs' constant drive for innovation, his deep mistrust of authority figures, and his ability to craft an elaborate vision, it makes sense to see he did well at an individual level, but struggled in a team environment.

Quote # 2

"Ultimately, it comes down to taste. It comes down to trying to expose yourself to the best things that humans have done and then try to bring those things into what you're doing. Picasso had a saying: good artists copy, great artists steal. And we have always been shameless about stealing great ideas, and I think part of what made the Macintosh great was that the people working on it were musicians and poets and artists and zoologists and historians who also happened to be the best computer scientists in the world."

Quote Context:

Interview with Steve Jobs for the 1995 documentary *Triumph of the Nerd: The Rise of Accidental Empires*. The documentary's stated goal was to show how "youthful amateurs, hippies, and self-proclaimed "nerds" accidentally changed the world."

Get to know Jobs:

After Jobs returned from his trip to India, Jobs and Wozniak picked up where they left off and started going to the Homebrew Computer Club together. One day, Wozniak shared the Apple I that he had invented. Not knowing much about engineering, Jobs was impressed, and felt there was an incredible opportunity in the marketplace for those interested in computers as a hobby. With all the engineers at Homebrew excited about Wozniak's computer, the two struck up a deal where Jobs would begin selling the product. At the time, with no place to work from, they began business out of Jobs' parents' garage.

Steve Wozniak writes,

> *"Steve had a good argument. We were in his car and he said — and I can remember him saying this like it was yesterday: "Well, even if we lose money, we'll have a company. For once in our lives, we'll have a company." That convinced me. And I was excited to think about us like that. To be two best friends starting a company."*

The name, Apple, wasn't the product of hours of creative brainstorming, but was simply reminiscent of a summer Jobs had spent at an apple orchard in Oregon.

After the Homebrew Computer Club got a sneak peek into what Jobs and Wozniak were up to, a local store agreed to support them by taking in 50 of the machines. Without the startup capital needed to finance their new venture, they raised money by selling Wozniak's HP calculator, and Jobs' Volkswagen microbus. When Wozniak finished his first computer, he began working on a new and improved edition. The Apple II that followed, although patterned after the Apple I, was still a significant breakthrough and created more excitement about what they were creating. Following the release of this model, the two realized they needed to secure more investment to continue. Jobs began chatting with a number of venture capitalists that were seemingly ubiquitous in California's Silicon Valley. Don Valentine was one of the first VCs they approached. Although he rejected the opportunity to invest in their venture, he recommended his friend Mike Markkula, who he said might be interested. Mike had worked for Intel, and at the young age of 34, was already worth millions. Mike helped the two create a business plan--his suggestion was an investment of $250,000 which would allow them to create

1,000 computers. Being as young and inexperienced as they were in the business world, this number seemed astronomical. In order to secure the deal, Wozniak left Hewlett Packard. While quitting his steady job was done somewhat reluctantly, as a caveat of the deal going through, he had no choice if he wanted to move forward.

In the spring of 1977, their growing company was preparing to present their product at the West Coast Computer Faire. While it was still a prototype, its professional, plastic case gave the Apple II the appeal and finesse of a finished product. Acting on the advice of Mike Markkula and Regis McKenna, Jobs purchased his first suit and got a prime booth in the heart of the action. At the show alone, they would go on to receive an incredible 300 orders, doubling the lifetime sales of the Apple I's. However, this was only a foreshadowing of what was to come. Over the next five years, revenue would grow exponentially, hitting $775,000 in 1977 and surpassing everyone's expectations by reaching $118 million by 1980.

Lesson from Steve Jobs:

While Jobs didn't have a big role in the programming and technical side of their products, he had a big picture perspective and an ability to get the right resources and people in place to transition a plan into reality. While his best friend undoubtedly created the first Apple product, Jobs is primarily credited with the success of the idea. By seeing the potential of what Wozniak had created, he pushed Wozniak to achieve things that may never have otherwise come to fruition. The genius of Jobs was truly his ability to look into the future, see the long-term potential of an idea, and move all the pieces into place to execute his plan.

Quote # 3

"I've done a lot of things I'm not proud of, such as getting my girlfriend pregnant when I was 23 and the way I handled that. But I don't have any skeletons in my closet that can't be allowed out."

Quote Context:

Quote made to 9to5Mac in 2011 by Steve Jobs about his biography *Steve Jobs*.

Get to know Jobs:

In 1977, one of Apple's now numerous employees, Rod Holt, hired Jobs' girlfriend to design and develop blueprints. Artistically gifted, it seemed like the ideal situation. Surprisingly, Brennan seemed reluctant to accept the position, and while it confused Holt at the time, it made sense: Brennan had recently found out she was pregnant.

Brennan was reluctant to tell Jobs about the pregnancy, and seemingly her fear was not unfounded. While he claimed he didn't want to ask her to get an abortion, he avoided any discussion of the situation and was unwilling to take on the responsibility of raising a child together. Frustrated by his complete lack of support, Brennan moved out. Getting an abortion was not her desire, but Brennan felt unequipped to deal with the situation, having separated from Jobs and also having a strained relationship with her parents. Holt, aware of their relationship disintegrating, was ignorant about why this would impact Brennan's decision to work alongside Jobs at Apple. Brennan quickly refused the offer to apprentice at her ex-boyfriend's company and moved on.

On an Oregon commune in 1978, Jobs' first daughter, Lisa, was born. Jobs continued to blatantly refuse any responsibility, not providing Brennan with any financial help and even going so far as to deny paternity of the baby. Forced to take on a cleaning job and apply for welfare, Brennan got by on her own for a while. Eventually, a court-ordered paternity test proved Jobs was the father, and a judge ordered Jobs to pay Brennan $385 per month. In addition to his child support payments, he was also required to repay for welfare that was previously drawn from the Oregon government.

After Apple went public leaving Jobs with a net worth of over $1 million, Jobs increased his contributions to $500 per month. Brennan, accepting an interview with *Time* magazine, disclosed a lot about their tumultuous relationship that was captured in the "Person of the Year" edition published later that fall. Jobs, also interviewed, still adamantly held to the fact that he may not be Lisa's father, purporting that the DNA test was only 94% accurate. In addition, he rejected the connection between the name of his daughter and LISA, which he defensively declared was simply an acronym for "Local Integrated Systems Architecture".

In January of 1983, *Time* took an interesting twist on its normal habit, and rather than naming Jobs the person of the year, it named the computer he had helped develop "the Machine of the Year".

Thankfully, Jobs later reconciled with both Brennan and his daughter Lisa. When she was nine, Lisa asked to change her last name from Brennan to Jobs, and her father gladly agreed, also acknowledging that the LISA was named after his daughter, and not just an acronym.

Lesson from Steve Jobs:

Jobs did many things that most people would not be proud of. He denied his daughter, failed to provide financial support to his child, and harassed and embarrassed employees. However, Jobs faced and came to grips with his shortcomings. He eventually made amends with his daughter and her mother In regards to his employees, he believed-- rightly or wrongly--that the ends justified the means. Berating those who worked with him was the price to be paid to get that final, beautiful product out of those that worked with him.

Quote # 4

"Do you want to spend the rest of your life selling sugared water, or do you want to come with me and change the world?"

Quote Context:

Steve Jobs in 1983 convincing John Sculley then President of Pepsi-Cola to move to Apple.

Get to know Jobs:

In the early 80s, fierce competition from the PC that IBM had developed threatened Apple's sales growth, so Jobs and his team responded by commencing work on a new project. Determined to complete the project, launching the Macintosh, Jobs mercilessly pushed his team members, demanding compliance and perfection. The way Jobs treated his team took a toll; over time, arguments and discussions erupted. While he may have been brilliant, his arrogance seemed to overshadow this at times. While Jobs believed putting people in their place would serve to spur them on to greatness, it often worked against him, his team members growing increasingly fearful of him, some avoiding him.

A previous vice president of the industrial design department at Apple stated that Jobs seemed to relieve stress by hurting those around him. Jobs seemed to feel entitled to treat others in a disrespectful or humiliating manner, and would do so on a regular basis. In addition, his emotional intelligence was used for evil sometimes, as he knew how to effectively wound those he was close to with extreme precision.

Jobs continued to press on towards his vision for the Macintosh, but he also decided having a more traditional face would help position the company in a way that would be more palatable to the corporate world. He set his sights on John Sculley, who at that time was CEO and President at Pepsi. Sculley was Pepsi's youngest-ever CEO and credited with helping the company achieve its top spot among competing pop brands. Getting Sculley to leave behind a secure, well-paid position where he was already doing incredibly well seemed like a big undertaking, however Jobs famously questioned Sculley whether he wanted to spend the rest of his life selling "sugared water," or join Jobs in "changing the world". Obviously, he chose the latter.

Evidently, Jobs had again achieved exactly what he wanted. Finely attuned to the motivations and psychological drivers of his peers, he was able to effectively convince Sculley to jump ship at Pepsi, a move that was largely unexpected. The two quickly developed a strong friendship and would eventually be referred to by *Business Week* as the "dynamic duo". Jobs' intuition about Sculley, and the need to find a convincing, corporate face for the company seemed to be right on, helping position Apple in a positive light among the media and in the corporate world alike.

Lesson from Steve Jobs:

The takeaway from Jobs' approach is that he was never satisfied. Having a vision for tackling any obstacle that came his way and achieve the impossible, he was relentless in his pursuit. When his peers or colleagues would put a damper on his plans, he ignored their advice. The work of his colleague Sculley, selling "sugared water," may have seemed like a safe and intelligent choice;

however Jobs was able to lure him over by crafting a future vision that was compelling, exciting and with endless possibility. Jobs always took a chance to try and achieve the impossible, even if that meant risking it all. In addition to his well-known charisma and inspiring nature, Jobs knew how to leverage his interpersonal skills to his advantage as well. On many occasions, he manipulated the feelings and emotions of his friends, colleagues and peers to get what he wanted. Opportunistic and cunning, he jumped at the chance to approach Sculley, who was in the midst of a successful career, yet seemingly not as fulfilled as he could have been. The right timing, combined with Jobs' ability to paint an intriguing future vision was able to secure him the perfect leverage to get what he wanted.

Quote # 5

"I think if you do something and it turns out pretty good, then you should go do something else wonderful, not dwell on it for too long. Just figure out what's next."

Quote Context:

2006 Steve Jobs interview with Brian Williams of NBC's *Nightly News*.

Get to know Jobs:

As time progressed, Sculley and Jobs' close friendship started to deteriorate. Having different visions, Sculley wanted to base the hardware on the Apple II, with open architecture and going after educational and home markets. On the other hand, Jobs felt closed architecture was the key in being able to compete with IBM's PC and go after the business market. While this was going on, Microsoft gave Apple an ultimatum, saying until they had free rein within their operating system, they wouldn't produce Mac applications. Acting as the CEO, Sculley agreed, giving Microsoft the software license for Mac's operating system; however, he underestimated the fallout and the backlash from Jobs. When IBM turned around to produce cheaper copies of the Macintosh, including graphic user interfaces, Jobs' anger grew. By the end of the 80s, IBM's marketing had outpaced Apple's and tension began to grow between Sculley and Jobs.

The organizational layout at Apple mirrored the tension building between the two, with Sculley managing the Apple II division and Jobs leading the Macintosh division. With communication breaking down, the two seemed to be operating in silos, and as a consequence, were duplicating efforts in areas where they could have been collaborating. In the early part of 1985, the situation came to head when during the annual meeting, Sculley's team, although producing 85% of sales, was completely glossed over. With tensions at an all time high, the company lost a number of employees after this situation, as they felt unappreciated and left out. Wozniak, voicing his concern that the company had been going downhill for the past few years, decided to sell the majority of his stock.

Sculley jumped on the situation, heading up a restructuring and providing Jobs with a proposal where he would take on the primary product development role. In an unexpected turn of events, Sculley then removed him from the Macintosh team completely and left him in a powerless role.

Feeling extremely resentful, Jobs fought back in an attempt to get Sculley out of the company, and after Sculley found out, he tried to talk to Jobs face to face about the betrayal. Jobs, angry at the entire situation, resigned. While he faced significant pushback from the board, Jobs made it clear his decision was not up for discussion, and consequently left his own company in 1985.

Life went on and the company kept pressing forward, even with Jobs gone. In December of 1992, Sculley described an exciting future for the Internet in a speech, and also made the executive decision to start building the company's computers to run on the PowerPC microprocessor, instead of the Intel architecture they were currently using. This turned out to be a fatal error; not only did the company's board not like this new way of doing things, but another terrible quarter and the fierce competition they continued to face from PC were too much to tolerate. In 1993, Sculley left the company as well.

Lesson from Steve Jobs:

Although the Apple II was responsible for 85% of the company's sales, Jobs wasn't ready to sit back and take a comfortable stance. Rather, he pushed the company to focus on the "next," and figure out a new and innovative product. With the leadership of the company not in alignment to his grandiose vision, Jobs was often perceived as being overly rebellious and challenging, causing dissention within the company. In a future interview, Sculley would admit this and mention that after Jobs kept bringing forward elaborate plans for the Macintosh division, the board asked him to step down. Jobs didn't want to conform to any limits and didn't believe in stifling his creativity and innovation. With his insistence on pushing the limits, he proved that he'd rather walk away from the company he had founded than compromise on his vision.

Quote # 6

"So when a good idea comes, you know, part of my job is to move it around, just see what different people think, get people talking about it, argue with people about it, get ideas moving among that group of 100 people, get different people together to explore different aspects of it quietly, and, you know - just explore things."

Quote Context:

Exclusive interview with Fortune senior editor Betsy Morris in February 2008, in Kona, Hawaii

Get to know Jobs:

While Jobs was heading up his division at Apple, he was still striking up connections within the realm of academia. During a luncheon celebrating the current President of France one day in Silicon Valley, Jobs met Paul Berg, who was a Nobel Laureate in Chemistry. After a lengthy discussion, Berg vented his frustrations about how costly it was to teach concepts such as genetics to students using textbooks rather than "wet laboratories". Because wet laboratories remained so expensive, they were completely out of a reach for an undergraduate classroom. Paul Berg made a suggestion that Jobs look into creating a "3M" computer to be applied within the higher education realm. Leaving the luncheon inspired with this new idea and a rapidly forming vision, Jobs started NeXT. Continuing to connect with Berg to garner feedback on the concept, he also sought input from other educational buyers. His vision for the company was to create a computer so powerful that it could effectively simulate the wet-lab environment, but would also be within financial reach for the average student.

Jobs' glory was short-lived however. Before the specifications were even complete, Apple found out and Jobs was quickly served with papers; Apple claimed Jobs had stolen their technology. Jobs countered, and voiced his amusement at the fact that a $2 billion company with over 4,000 employees would be wasting their time on a small startup of "six people in blue jeans." Luckily for Jobs, the lawsuit was dismissed before going to trial; however, the lawsuit had resulted in a significant amount of momentum being lost. For the first year, Jobs' new company was unable to work on any specific products, as they feared losing the trial and having to provide their work to Apple. However, Jobs used this time wisely, planning and thinking strategically about how he could build a solid and successful company.

One of Jobs' talents seemed to be leveraging the right people to work on a project. With his keen sense of finding a good fit, he consistently bragged that he would only hire the best and the brightest. With even their receptionist having a Ph.D., there was a lot of excitement and buzz surrounding the new startup. Although working for NeXT was perhaps considered a risky move, as no specific roles or performance measures had yet been defined, it was a highly sought-after place to work. Avie Tevanian was one of these talented recruits that NeXT was able to snag. Still a student at the time, Avie was incredibly gifted in software development. His current project was a UNIX kernel named Mach. Consistent with his ability to captivate others with his charismatic and visionary approach, Jobs told Avie to imagine running his invention on millions of computers within a few years' time. This could be possible if only he would join NeXT.

NeXT had an interesting financial model, which

remained distinct from any other companies within Silicon Valley at the time. Two salary levels meant you would either earn $75,000 in a senior role, or simply the $50,000 everyone else received. NeXT also offered a variety of benefits - from memberships at the health club to emergency loans and free juice, it gave the company that startup feel that Silicon Valley is now well known for. With all this in place, the company was still funded by Steve Jobs, with no significant revenue coming in during these early years.

Money was spent freely to get only the best in return. Needing a corporate brand, Jobs asked his network to refer him to the best logo designer "on the planet." Paul Rand, a Yale Art Professor, designed the NeXT logo for $100K, which supposedly stood for 'education, excellence, expertise, exceptional, excitement, e=mc2...'

When it came to NeXT's headquarters, no expense seemed to be spared either. One of the first employees was Tom Carlisle, who was working full time as an interior designer. After settling in one of Silicon Valley's most prestigious areas, Carlisle upgraded the house to have beautiful glass walls and Ansel Adams prints throughout. Hardwood floors extended throughout the house to a luxurious kitchen with granite countertops and a sitting area with huge U-shaped sofas.

Unsurprisingly, as the year went on, the company, still without revenue, found its funds rapidly depleting and the product was still far from its launch date. With a need for funding, Jobs was lucky to stumble across billionaire Ross Perot. With a significant investment, the NeXT computer launched at an extravagant, invite-only gala in the Louise M. Davies Symphony Hall on October 12, 1988.

Lesson from Steve Jobs:

While the NeXT Computer may not have been a huge success from a revenue standpoint, it illustrated Jobs' willingness to take calculated risks in order to achieve his vision for the future. Successful entrepreneurs know the importance of understanding their strengths and weaknesses, and then finding and hiring people who are "better" than they are. While teamwork was an area that Jobs undoubtedly struggled with, he was able to successfully paint that big picture and lead others to accomplish things they never thought were possible. Leveraging the talents and motivation of his staff to accomplish a common vision was key in his success, and Jobs had an innate ability to pull all the pieces in place to make things happen.

Quote # 7

"Getting fired from Apple was the best thing that could have ever happened to me. The heaviness of being successful was replaced by the lightness of being a beginner again. It freed me to enter one of the most creative periods of my life."

Quote Context:

2005 Steve Jobs Commencement Speech at Stanford University

Get to know Jobs:

After leaving Apple in 1986, besides NeXT, Jobs invested nearly $10 million for The Graphics Group to create Pixar. Being part of the Lucasfilm computer division founded in 1971 by filmmaker George Lucas, Pixar started as a hardware company, but was more renowned for its CGI-animated films. With slow sales threatening Pixar's success, a division was created in 1989 with the goal to approach private companies and create computer-animated commercials as a way of increasing profits. After a number of incredibly successful projects for major brands such as Tropicana, Listerine and Life Savers, the company decided to sell the original hardware division and pivot their efforts to animation only. With this sale occurring in the spring of 1989, they didn't know that only two short years later, they would strike a $26 million deal with Disney to produce three computer-animated feature films. Starting out with Toy Story in 1995, Pixar would produce a huge variety of famous computer-animated films over the next decade, including a number that received Academy Awards for Best Animated Feature. From major hits like A Bug's Life,

Monsters Inc. or Finding Nemo, Pixar forever changed the animated movie industry. Looking back, it's fascinating to know this success may have never come to be if Jobs had not resigned from Apple.

Lesson from Steve Jobs:

Jobs didn't do well when he was being evaluated based on simply revenue or losses. When Jobs left Apple, he was able to apply his creativity and innovation to a completely different sector that was desperately calling for change. Jobs illustrated how it can be more beneficial to step away from something that's becoming too mundane and focus energy elsewhere. With a new opportunity and a different perspective, we can experience a burst of creativity that wouldn't have otherwise occurred. Jobs always held true to his innovative spirit and desire to break the mold, and consequently, he wasn't willing to waste his energy in a place that was holding him back. Likewise, anyone can apply this lesson and refuse to be held back by rules or constraints. Instead, always press on and be driven by your intuition and vision, and you'll undoubtedly experience success as a by-product of simply applying your talents and doing what you love.

Quote # 8

"I'm convinced that about half of what separates successful entrepreneurs from the non-successful ones is pure perseverance."

Quote Context:

1995 Steve Jobs interview by Daniel Morrow of Computerworld Information Technology Awards Foundation as part of their oral history project.

Get to know Jobs:

A press release in 1996 came as a surprise to many: Apple was purchasing NeXT for $429 million. Apple claimed the goal in acquiring NeXTSTEP was a means to transition Mac's operating system, which was quickly becoming dated. However, keeping in mind the struggle Apple had faced over the previous decade in their fierce rivalry with Microsoft, many thought this decision to purchase was driven by a desire to change their public image.

In early 1997, after the completion of the purchase, Jobs returned to Apple, but as a consultant this time. When the current Apple CEO, Gil Amelio, was let go, Jobs became the acting CEO. In his new role, Jobs began a concerted effort to get the company to a more successful spot. His first move was to talk to each pocket of the company. Jobs asked every product team to justify their role in the company and explain exactly how the product they were working on was contributing to the company's success. Non-profitable products would be rigorously questioned and in many cases, the team was dismissed. The previous CEO, Amelio, had already begun to make cuts and identify areas for greater efficiency within the company. In the few months before he was dismissed, Amelio had cut close to 300 projects that were being worked on, leaving the company with about 50 product teams. After Jobs completed his evaluations, only about 10 product teams remained. In the months that followed, employees were afraid of spontaneously encountering Jobs. While riding the elevator, they feared they might be fired when the elevator doors opened. While it was uncommon for someone to be randomly fired, the situation that had just happened and the whittling down of the project teams was enough to keep the entire company on edge.

Steve Jobs first set his sights on the pro products, including the Power Mac and PowerBook, which were launched in the fall of 1997. Sales were good, which reaffirmed Jobs' beliefs about Apple's target market. He seemed aware that many Mac buyers had avoided new purchases over the past couple years with the underlying fear that Apple wouldn't make it. Once Jobs rejoined the company and was able to quell some of the fears surrounding Apple, sales began to rise. In 1998, Jobs proudly declared at Macworld that the company was profitable again, and as year 2000 arrived, he officially became Apple's CEO.

The purchase of NeXT had created the right conditions for Apple to be able to create the OS X operating system. Jobs' proud return to Apple had completely changed the direction of the company and positioned it for success. His speech at Macworld was a huge turning point. It was the perfect time for Jobs to become the official CEO. His work at Pixar may have been in jeopardy if he had accepted this role sooner. Rather than being CEO of two public companies at the same time, Jobs waited until his role at Pixar had changed.

Now, with Pixar being successfully managed by Ed Catmull and John Lasseter, and having recently launched two highly successful movies, Jobs could confidently begin to focus the majority of his energy on running Apple. In his time as interim CEO, Jobs had changed the game and positioned Apple as an innovative industry leader once again. His news was well received. With significant applause and cheering, it was evident that the company's fans and stakeholders were relieved to hear of Apple's revival and were excited for what the future held.

Lesson from Steve Jobs:

Often, Jobs would pursue his goals with little regard for collateral damage or the consequences of his actions. Pushing his way to the top, he undoubtedly felt that the end justified the means. Equipped with a vision or struck with an idea, he would put the onus on one of his people to simply "make it happen". He had little tolerance for being challenged or argued with, and certainly didn't accept those who identified barriers to his success or claimed something was impossible. Jobs was also willing to try things and take a "wait and see" approach to whether it would pan out. If products or plans didn't end up performing as Jobs had envisioned, he was quick to move on and cut his losses. Consequently, his approach was highly agile and refreshingly non-corporate. While some may argue his success could be credited to his stubborn arrogance more than his reputation as a determined visionary, his approach undoubtedly worked. Strong willed and perseverant, Jobs refused to take no for an answer and had the tenacity to push forward when faced with continuous challenges.

Quote # 9

"Innovation distinguishes between a leader and a follower

Quote Context:

"The Innovation Secrets of Steve Jobs," 2001

Get to know Jobs:

In 1987, Jobs was involved in a very public-facing debate with Michael Dell, who was working as Dell Computer's CEO at the time. The feud ensured after Jobs made a statement that Dell simply created "un-innovative beige boxes." In 1997 at the Garter Symposium, Michael Dell had been asked to provide his input into Apple's troubled situation in that time. His answer, "I'd shut it down and give the money back to the shareholders," not only demonstrated their highly opposite approaches to business, but also brought to light an underlying sense of contempt they seemed to have for each other.

In many ways, Michael Dell was the arch-nemesis of Jobs. Using the Intel computer in the 80s as a student, Dell had completely transformed the approach for selling computers. Dell had previously stated that Apple's shareholders would be "better off" should the company go under. Jobs had added fuel to the fire by going as far as painting a bulls-eye on a Dell photo at a Macworld exhibition. In a public and ongoing war of words, it seemed to go beyond the professional and showcase a personal feud between the two. Dell publicly predicted Apple would experience impending failure; in return, Jobs used a boxy portable Dell computer to show off the features of

Apple's sleek new iBook. At every opportunity, these two leaders would disparage and criticize the other.

Facing a marked decrease in computer sales among the consumer market, the passionate rivalry continued. From the early 90s to 2001, Apple dropped from the top spot in the computer industry to the sixth. With Jobs' return to the company, Apple was again positioned as the creative and perhaps risky choice, whereas Dell was branded as the reliable, traditional choice that didn't deviate from the norm.

While both Jobs and Dell were obviously industry leaders, they didn't share much else in common. A Harvard Business School professor, David Yoffie once explained that Job and Dell represented different generations. With Jobs being a child of the 60s and 70s, he valued counterculture and challenging the status quo. Dell, coming from the Reagan 80s, seemed to fit in more with the traditional conservative Republican businessman.

Andrew Heller, a previous IBM computer designer and investor out of Texas, talked about Dell's role as a "pioneer," in changing the way consumers purchase. Dell had completely changed the game by allowing online computer sales and creating highly organized systems that would allow for streamlined manufacturing and shipment within a few hours. Jobs, on the other hand, had a talent for shaping exactly "what" the consumers wanted to buy. Heller claimed this was the main reason why Dell was enjoying the stability of a reliable job as an executive, whereas Jobs' career had been much more tumultuous.

Perhaps there was a sense of envy on the part of both Dell and Jobs, Yoffie suggested. Dell undoubtedly lacked the creativity and the cutting-edge flair that Apple exhibited. In addition, it seemed Jobs was always in the limelight, capturing the attention of the media and stakeholders alike. Meanwhile, Apple seemed unequipped in figuring out how to achieve the elusive market growth that Dell had experienced.

In 2006, when Apple's market capital went above Dell's, Jobs sent an email to his employees to mark the occasion:

> *Team, it turned out that Michael Dell wasn't perfect at predicting the future. Based on today's stock market close, Apple is worth more than Dell. Stocks go up and down, and things may be different tomorrow, but I thought it was worth a moment of reflection today. Steve.*

Lesson from Steve Jobs:

The bitter rivalry between Jobs and Dell seemed to only spur Jobs on to achieve greater success. Even when others had lost faith in his approach or his company, he knew what he was capable of and held true to his future vision. His unrelenting desire to prove others wrong gave him an unparalleled motivation to strive towards achievement. Even in the face of competition, Jobs didn't give up. For those in the business world, this lesson holds true. Those who are unafraid to forge their own path, to be relentless in their pursuit of innovation, are the ones that will succeed and become the leaders. Dell's brand, while reliable, positioned them as a company that followed, rather than Apple's name for leading a completely new path. As Dell's approach seemed to run so counter to everything Jobs believed in, it makes sense why the rivalry took place.

Quote #10

"You can't just ask customers what they want and then try to give that to them. By the time you get it built, they'll want something new."

Quote Context:

Quote made to Inc. magazine in 1989 when the magazine named him Entrepreneur of the Decade.

Get to know Jobs:

There was undoubtedly a lot of secrecy surrounding Apple's products. Prior to the iPhone's release, most of the company seemed to be completely in the dark. The majority of Apple's employees weren't even aware of the details, not whether it was a phone or a television. Rumors claimed that senior employees at the company would drink Scotch as they fearfully watched the iPhone launch demo, dreading the moment their prototype might unexpectedly fail during a presentation.

One of the engineers claimed that the designers had a significant amount of pull at the company, being thought of as "artists". The first iPhone design, of completely brushed aluminum, left engineers struggling to explain the concept of radio waves to Jobs and his top designers, describing the design as a "beautiful brick," that would trap these waves from escaping.

Initially presented in San Francisco, tensions were high among the development team. The iPhone's development process had involved arguments, disagreements and a lack of sleep. Taking the incomplete prototype on stage was a risk; while it could play a small selection of music, the phone would crash if the full file were played. Apps followed suit; they could be opened, but there was a high probability they could crash in front of the captive audience. Engineers and managers sat on the edge of their seats, and when the presentation ended without any hiccups, there was a collective sigh of relief among the Apple employees.

Following the iPhone's release in 2007, Apple was positioned as a leading newcomer to the cellular phone industry. It offered a multi-touch display phone with the features of an iPod and completely transformed the business sector with its mobile browsing capabilities. Jobs believed in innovation above all, but he also was quoted as saying "real artists ship." He knew the team could have worked on the iPhone forever in their pursuit of perfection, but there was a point where "shipping it" was imperative and secured the company its role as an industry leader. Over the upcoming years, Apple went on to release nine generations of iPhone models.

The success of the iPhone has transformed the smartphone sector and positioned Apple was one of the most valuable public companies in the world. One of the first phones to offer a slate format and touchscreen usability, the majority of future smartphones followed suit. As of 2015, the iPhone held an incredible 44% of the smartphone market share in the U.S. alone.

Lesson from Steve Jobs:

Jobs had a passion and a drive to create things that people didn't even know they wanted yet. As a true innovator, he didn't simply improve upon an already existing product, but truly went outside the boundaries of what was thought to be possible and created something completely unique. Jobs had an innate ability to challenge the status quo and reimagine an existing product. With Jobs at the helm, Apple positioned itself as a frontrunner in the industry and showcased its ability to transform the way society thought about communication.

Quote # 11

"Being the richest man in the cemetery doesn't matter to me. ... Going to bed at night saying we've done something wonderful ... that's what matters to me."

Quote Context:

1993 interview with *The Wall Street Journal*. Jobs was commenting on the success of Bill gates and Microsoft. Steve Jobs did not originate the saying. The earliest evidence of this general expression was when a popular comedian, Ed Wynn, was interviewed in January 1932.

Get to know Jobs:

At the young age of 23, Jobs had a net worth of

$1M dollars, which would rise to over $250M within two years. Only a few people have landed themselves a spot on the Forbes list of the nation's richest without inherited wealth, and Jobs not only accomplished this, but also was one of the youngest to do so.

In 2011, when Jobs passed away, he had a net worth of $10.2 billion. However, in contrast to Bill Gates' worth of $79.4 billion (2016) when Apple is worth incredibly more than both Microsoft and Google, at first glance this seems strange. Further investigation shows that Jobs sold his shares at Apple when leaving the company and again in 1997 to illustrate his distrust in the current Apple CEO, Gil Amelio. Some may consider this sale to be an emotional, perhaps reckless decision--if Jobs had decided to keep the 11% stake he had in the company back in the 80s, he would have been worth at least $54 billion when he passed away.

After his return to Apple in 1997, Jobs apparently put an end to the company's philanthropic efforts in a move to decrease their costs. Many have purported that these programs were never reinstated, with a *Wired* article claiming that Jobs was notably missing from the Giving USA's list for the past four years, in spite of his net worth. One quote described Jobs as a "greedy" capitalist, stating that he doesn't even support causes with a deep meaning to him. For example, as a cancer survivor, it would be expected he would have the desire to support these types of charities. In a 1985 interview, Jobs claimed it takes a lot of time to contribute money, as with philanthropy, there isn't a measurement system, so it makes evaluating your success impossible. However, he claimed when he had additional time, he would start a public foundation.

This claim was fulfilled when Jobs began a

charitable foundation in the late 80s. However, as suddenly as it began, he closed it only 15 months later. The manager of the foundation at the time claimed Jobs didn't have the time to ensure the foundation's success. One of his close friends said Jobs felt he could do more good simply by working on the expansion of his company. Of course, this is not without merit; if Jobs had spent the last decade of his life giving money away, rather than using his energy to invent and innovate, how would our society be different?

Perhaps we may not have the ability to scroll through our latest emails on a mobile device, or look up something on the Internet at a moment's notice. The iPad may have been a distant dream--a product that's been implemented across the health, educational and medical sectors to do everything from sharing medical information in real time to teaching special needs children. While Jobs may not have been a renowned philanthropist, he has undoubtedly revolutionized the way we communicate and improved the lives of many people across the globe.

In addition, Jobs seemed to be a very private person at times--it is very possible donations were made, but simply in a private or anonymous way. As a famed individual who ran the most profitable company in the world, we know surprisingly little about his home life, the relationship with his wife, Laurene Powell, or his four children. Other than the basic information, much of the details surrounding Jobs' personal life are unknown. His personality was an interesting mix, exhibiting some traits that seemed to run completely counter to others. When in the public eye, launching his products, Jobs was excited, charismatic, inspiring and had an incredible ability to make others laugh. In other situations, he could be withdrawn, quiet and distant.

Mike Randazzo, an analyst in the business and tech sector, claimed that Steve Jobs was an incredibly private individual. Randazzo once remarked that while it wasn't commonly reported in mainstream media, Jobs was an extremely shy person, and had an intense need for privacy. Outside of the limelight, a few close individuals knew Jobs as a philanthropist. While they may not have been public, friends have spoken about over $50 million being donated to hospitals in Stanford, and a variety of projects in the battle against AIDS. With a desire to keep his personal life under wraps, he donated out of a desire to help, rather than be praised for his philanthropy.

Lesson from Steve Jobs:

Steve Jobs never seemed to be driven by money. Instead of being known for his financial status, Jobs sought to be recognized for the innovative products and the unique inventions he created, and the benefit they offered the world. Rather than focusing on profit, he pressed on in his passion to create, and the money shortly came.

Quote # 12

"For the past 33 years, I have looked in the mirror every morning and asked myself: 'If today were the last day of my life, would I want to do what I am about to do today?' And whenever the answer has been 'No' for too many days in a row, I know I need to change something."

Quote Context:

2005 Steve Jobs Commencement Address at Stanford University.

Getting to know Jobs:

Jobs found out in the fall of 2003 that he had pancreatic cancer. In general, pancreatic cancer offers a slim chance of survival. Even with this diagnosis, Jobs ignored his doctors' recommendations for close to nine months. Rather than being treated in a traditional way, he started to use alternative medicine and homeopathic treatments, in addition to changing his diet. Whether these choices impacted his health for better or worse continues to be a controversial topic.

Ramzi Amri, a Harvard medical researcher, feels that Jobs' use of alternative treatment, rather than following traditional channels, caused him to have an "unnecessarily early death". Others adamantly disagree with Amri's viewpoint. David Gorski, a cancer researcher and alternative medicine critic, believes Jobs' survival was only affected minimally. Others, such as Barrie R. Cassileth, Chief of Integrative Medicine at Memorial Sloan Kettering Cancer Center, go as far as saying that

Jobs basically committed suicide, as the type of pancreatic cancer he was diagnosed with was treatable and curable through traditional medicine.

Jobs' biographer, Walter Isaacson, speaks about his decision to refuse surgery for his cancer, and claims Jobs later regretted the decision as his health continued declining. Rather than undergo surgery, Jobs followed a vegan diet, underwent acupuncture treatments, and used herbal remedies. A holistic doctor that Jobs had grown to trust recommended he do bowl cleansings and juicing fasts. Jobs seemed to put a solid effort into trying a variety of alternative treatments before he gave in and underwent his surgery in 2004. Over the summer, his pancreaticoduodenectomy, also known as the Whipple procedure, was successful in getting the tumor removed, although Jobs continued to refuse chemotherapy or radiation.

Throughout Jobs' medical leave, Tim Cook, previously head of sales and operations, managed the company.

In August of that year, Jobs attended the Worldwide Developers Conference to deliver the keynote speech on behalf of Apple. His appearance shocked the audience; thin and pale, he lacked his renowned charisma and enthusiasm. In addition, others were delegated to deliver other sections of the keynote, which created relentless rumors about Jobs' health. Apple's spokesperson at the time released a short statement claiming that his health was "robust".

Two years later, rumors surfaced again following Jobs' speech at the WWDC. Again, Apple denied the rumors, claiming that Jobs had simply caught a cold. Others claimed that the previous Whipple procedure had no doubt left him gaunt and listless. In July, during a conference call to discuss

Apple's earnings, Jobs was peppered with questions about his health and appearance. Reiterating that his health was a private matter, he also faced criticism from shareholders who felt they were not being informed properly. The *New York Times* finally stated that although obviously his health issues were not simply due to a cold, they also weren't life or death, and his cancer had not returned.

Although common for newspapers to retain an inventory of obituaries for famous people so publishing can happen immediately following any news, *Bloomberg* accidentally published Jobs obituary in August of 2008. Although the obituary contained blank spaces for the years and age, and was immediately redacted, the media exploded and the situation only fueled the speculation about Jobs' health. Jobs seemed to take these rumors in stride, even making jokes. At a keynote address, he quoted Mark Twain, joking, "Reports of my death are greatly exaggerated." At another event, his final slide simply said "110/70", alluding to his healthy and normal blood pressure. He then stated that no additional questions about his health would be answered.

In December, Apple surprisingly released a statement that Phil Schiller, VP of Marketing, would deliver the final speech at the Macworld Conference. Rumors resurfaced once again, and by early January, Apple stated that Jobs' health was indeed declining, due to a "hormone imbalance" that he'd been battling for a number of months.

The following year, in 2009, Jobs shared in a memo that his health issues were "more complex" than he previously believed. At this point, he had decided to go on a medical leave of six months. Although he would still be involved in directing the company's strategy and playing a role in large decisions, this would allow him to focus on getting better. Following this announcement, Cook once again became the acting CEO.

Cook, who shared the same blood type as Jobs, offered to donate a portion of his liver. Jobs said he would never agree to that--however, faced with his declining health, he eventually consented and underwent a liver transplant that spring in Tennessee. Following the transplant, doctors told him his prognosis was excellent.

After returning to work that fall, Jobs would go on another medical leave only 18 months later. A letter to employees stated that this leave was so Jobs could focus more on his health. Similar to the previous leave, Cook once again resumed as interim CEO, with the plan for Jobs to be involved in company direction and major strategy.

However, on August 24, Jobs officially resigned. In his brief letter to the board of directors, he stated: "I have always said if there ever came a day when I could no longer meet my duties and expectations as Apple's CEO, I would be the first to let you know. Unfortunately, that day has come."

Jobs passed away in his home in Palo Alto, surrounded by family on October 5, 2011.

Lesson from Steve Jobs:

A common thread throughout the life of Steve Jobs was his desire to seek fulfillment. As a young twenty-something, Jobs headed to India to discover his purpose and throughout his tumultuous career, he always followed his passion. Steve Jobs wasn't afraid to take a risk, and if a job wasn't providing him with the rewards and fulfillment he sought, he was quick to cut his losses and move on. Having a huge vision for the future, and working tirelessly to fulfill these dreams, Jobs was always moving on to the next challenge or the next innovation. His mission in life was to create an impact in the world, as the man said himself, "I want to put a ding in the universe". Undoubtedly, he was successful in achieving this. Even with his failing health and knowing he had limited time, Jobs continued to work towards accomplishing his dream. Today, Jobs' impact on the world is still felt. Apple continues to be one of the most renowned and recognized companies across the globe, and Jobs' legacy continues to live on.

Quote #13

"You can't connect the dots looking forward; you can only connect them looking backward. So you have to trust that the dots will somehow connect in your future. You have to trust in something — your gut, destiny, life, karma, whatever. This approach has never let me down, and it has made all the difference in my life."

Quote Context:

2005 Steve Jobs Commencement Speech at Stanford University.

Conclusion

Jobs was always searching for the next adventure. He was always pushing the envelope, challenging the status quo and taking whatever risks he needed to in order to accomplish his dream. He was notably unapologetic about the effort he put in, even if some of his work was fruitless. Throughout his life, Jobs always sought to know more, to find out as much as he could and to find completely unique solutions for age-old questions. He had a "hunger" for more, and he let this guide every decision in his life.

Jobs was fearless about the risks. Of course, he made many mistakes and bad decisions, but always thought about what he could learn from them, rather than focusing on the negative. Instead of being held back by fear, or the opinions of others, he relished the challenge of jumping headfirst into a project that may very well result in failure. In the business world, people can let fear hold them back from accomplishing what they were meant to do. Whether deciding to open a company or launch a product, we can let fear paralyze us and hold us back, or we can cast fear away and push forward.

Jobs had an unparalleled self-confidence that propelled him towards success. Unafraid to forge a path that nobody else seemed to believe in, he trusted himself to make the right decision in the right moment. While some of his choices may have seemed questionable at the time, he let his intuition guide him, which often led to incredible accomplishments. Ahead of his time, he stayed unconstrained by industry norms, societal expectations and the negativity of others. While his life was an intriguing mix of twists and turns, each decision and every step along the way led to a result that may not have otherwise happened. Jobs believed we can only connect the dots when looking back, and his life certainly holds true to this statement. As Jobs always advocated, don't settle. take risks, and believe in the future. Stay Hungry. Stay Foolish.

Thank you for purchasing this book and reading it this far. I hope you have learned something valuable from the great Apple founder, Steve Jobs.

Finally, if you enjoyed this book, then I'd like to ask you for a favor, would you be kind enough to leave a review for this book on Amazon? Tell us what you like or dislike and what we can improve. Your feedbacks will be greatly appreciated!

https://www.amazon.com/dp/B01LYICYK4

Also follow EntrepreneurshipFacts on social media to stay updated with our new books and increase your knowledge about business and successful people on a daily basis:

Instagram   Facebook   Twitter

Check out our website for the latest facts and articles about business and entrepreneurship:

www.EntrepreneurshipFacts.com

More books by Entrepreneurship Facts

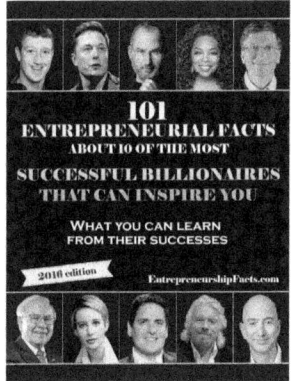

101 Entrepreneurial Facts About 10 of The Most Successful BILLIONAIRES That Can Inspire You: What you can learn from their successes

The Real Life RICH DAD & The Lessons He Taught ROBERT KIYOSAKI about Money

Warren Buffett - 41 Fascinating Facts about Life & Investing Philosophy: The Lessons From A Legendary Investor

Elon Musk - Top 10 Business Lessons Through An Inspiring Life Of A Visionary Entrepreneur:

DONALD TRUMP - Top 5 Business Lessons From The Presidential Campaign Of A Businessman: The Art Of Getting Attention

Richard Branson - Top 13 Secrets To Success in Life & Business: A Virgin Entrepreneur

www.ingramcontent.com/pod-product-compliance
Lightning Source LLC
Chambersburg PA
CBHW060404190526
45169CB00002B/741